REASONS TO CARE ABOUT
MARINE TURTLES
[Animals in Peril]

Sara Cohen Christopherson

Enslow Publishers, Inc.
40 Industrial Road
Box 398
Berkeley Heights, NJ 07922
USA
http://www.enslow.com

Library of Congress Cataloguing-in-Publication Data
Christopherson, Sara Cohen.
   Top 50 reasons to care about marine turtles : animals in peril / by Sara Cohen Christopherson.
      p. cm. — (Top 50 reasons to care about endangered animals)
   Includes bibliographical references and index.
   Summary: "Readers will learn about marine turtles—their life cycles, diets, young, habitats, and reasons why they are endangered animals"—Provided by publisher.
   ISBN 978-0-7660-3455-6
   1. Sea turtles—Juvenile literature. 2. Endangered species—Juvenile literature. I. Title. II. Title: Top fifty reasons to care about marine turtles.
   QL666.C536C47 2009
   597.92'8—dc22
                           2009010555

Printed in the United States of America

092009 Lake Book Manufacturing, Inc., Melrose Park, IL

10 9 8 7 6 5 4 3 2 1

To Our Readers: We have done our best to make sure all Internet Addresses in this book were active and appropriate when we went to press. However, the author and the publisher have no control over and assume no liability for the material available on those Internet sites or on other Web sites they may link to. Any comments or suggestions can be sent by e-mail to comments@enslow.com or to the address on the back cover.

♻ Enslow Publishers, Inc., is committed to printing our books on recycled paper. The paper in every book contains 10% and 30% post-consumer waste (PCW). The cover board on the outside of each book contains 100% PCW. Our goal is to do our part to help young people and the environment too!

Photographs: Jan Rysavy/iStockphoto, cover inset, 1; Peter Heiss/iStockphoto, 1; Ryan Saul/iStockphoto, 4; Alexey Stiop/iStockphoto, 6 (bottom); Philip Seys/iStockphoto, 6 (middle); Doug Perrine/Nature Picture Library, 6 (top), 14, 17, 22 (bottom), 34 (top), 40, 43, 61, 85, 93; John Cancalosi/iStockphoto, 8; Stephan Kerkhofs/iStockphoto, 11; YaQi Li/iStockphoto, 12; Loh Siew Seong/iStockphoto, 15; Jurgen Freund/Nature Picture Library, 18, 28, 37, 62, 83; Bullit Marquez/AP Images, 21; Andrea Gingerich/iStockphoto, 22 (top); Pete Oxford/Nature Picture Library, 24, 58; Red Line Editorial, 25, 29, 33; T.J. Rich/Nature Picture Library, 27, 50; Brent Hedges/Nature Picture Library, 30; Wai Chiew Ng/iStockphoto, 32; Carsten Madsen/iStockphoto, 34 (bottom); Georgette Douwma/Nature Picture Library, 36; Richard Carey/iStockphoto, 39; iStockphoto, 44; Frank Schoettke/iStockphoto, 46; Tammy Peluso/iStockphoto, 48; Jeanne Hatch/iStockphoto, 49; Aris Vidalis/iStockphoto, 52; Matthew Maran/Nature Picture Library, 53; Willem Kolvoort/Nature Picture Library, 55; Svitlana Prada/iStockphoto, 56; Ingo Arndt/Nature Picture Library, 57; Attila Pohlmann/iStockphoto, 65; Michael Freeman/Corbis, 66; Hanne & Jens Eriksen/Nature Picture Library, 69; Brian Wathen/iStockphoto, 71; Luis Castaneda/Photolibrary, 72; Miles Barton/Nature Picture Library, 74; Terence Mendoza/iStockphoto, 75; Jose B. Ruiz/Nature Picture Library, 76; Georgette DouwmaNature Picture Library, 79; Peter Bennett and Ursula Keuper-Bennett, 80; NOAA, 82; James Tutor/iStockphoto, 86; John Anderson/iStockphoto, 89; N.J. Tangkepayung/AP Images, 90; Valerie Loiseleux/iStockphoto, 94; Scott R. Benson/AP Images, 97; Ron Masessa/iStockphoto, 99

The image on p. 80 is courtesy of Peter Bennett and Ursula Keuper-Bennett. It was previously published in their book, *The Book of Honu: Enjoying and Learning About Hawaii's Sea Turtles* (Honolulu: University of Hawaii Press, 2008).

Cover caption: A hawksbill turtle swims near the Cayman islands in the Caribbean Sea.
Peter Heiss/iStockphoto

CONTENTS

ENDANGERED MARINE TURTLES

For thousands of years, humans have paid tribute to marine turtles in legend and in art. In many cultures around the world, turtles have been revered as a symbol, eaten as a delicacy, and admired for their beauty.

Marine turtles are remarkable creatures. Although they move slowly on land, most marine turtles travel thousands of miles across oceans to lay their eggs. Right after they hatch, marine turtles face an incredible journey. Baby turtles must dig out of their nests, avoid predators, and crawl across the beach to the ocean. Life—even after reaching the water—is so dangerous for a baby turtle that only about one in one thousand hatchlings will reach adulthood.

Today, all marine turtles are protected in the United States under the Endangered Species Act and are listed on the International Union for the Conservation of Nature (IUCN) Red List of Threatened Species. Human activities are the greatest threat to marine turtles. Turtles can be injured or killed by fishing gear and pollution. Coastal development interferes with turtle nesting sites. With human protection, marine turtles might have a chance at survival.

◀ MARINE TURTLES ARE THREATENED WITH EXTINCTION.

GETTING TO KNOW MARINE TURTLES

REASON TO CARE # 1

Marine Turtles
Are at Risk

Marine turtles are ocean-dwelling reptiles. After hatching, they spend almost their entire lives at sea. They come to the surface to breathe air. Only females return to land, leaving the water to lay eggs.

Marine turtles are divided into seven species: leatherback, green, hawksbill, loggerhead, olive ridley, Kemp's ridley, and flatback. All marine turtles are considered at risk of extinction. This book tells the stories of three species of marine turtles: leatherback, green, and hawksbill.

◄ TOP: LEATHERBACK TURTLE. MIDDLE: GREEN TURTLE. BOTTOM: HAWKSBILL TURTLE.

REASON TO CARE # 2

Marine Turtles Are Ancient

The first reptiles lived about 300 million years ago. These reptiles gave rise to land turtles and later to sea turtles. The earliest marine turtles swam the oceans more than 100 million years ago.

Some ancient sea turtles were gigantic. The Archelon sea turtle lived more than 70 million years ago. It measured 13 feet (4 meters) from head to tail. These ancient turtles lived among the dinosaurs. Although the dinosaurs did not survive the mass extinction that occurred 65 million years ago, some sea turtles did. These turtles were the ancestors of today's sea turtles.

[Scientists found the most complete fossils of the Archelon in the 1970s in South Dakota. Although now dry, water covered that area long ago.]

◄ THIS FOSSIL IS FROM AN ANCIENT TURTLE THAT LIVED BETWEEN 55 AND 34 MILLION YEARS AGO.

Marine Turtles
Have Many Names

Every organism has one scientific name. The first part of a scientific name is the genus. Many different species can belong to the same genus. The second part of the name is called the specific epithet. Each species has its own specific epithet. The green turtle is *Chelonia mydas*, the hawksbill turtle is *Eretmochelys imbricata*, and the leatherback turtle is *Dermochelys coriacea*.

[*Dermo* means "skin" and *chelys* means "tortoise." This name describes the skin-like shell of the leatherback.]

Each species can have many common names. The green turtle gets its name from the green-colored fat found under its shell. The hawksbill is named for the pointed hawk-like shape of its beak. The leatherback is named for its leathery shell.

[The Hawaiian word for turtle is *honu*. Green turtles are called *honu*. The word for a hawksbill is *'ea*.]

▶ THE HAWKSBILL HAS A POINTED BEAK SIMILAR TO THE BEAK OF A HAWK.

REASON TO CARE # 4

All Turtles Have Shells

Every turtle has a shell. Land turtles can pull their heads and limbs into their shells for protection or if startled. Unlike many land turtles, marine turtles cannot hide in their shells. Their heads and flippers are fixed out of the shell in a way that allows the turtles to swim.

The shells of all marine turtles are rigid and bony—with the exception of the leatherback. The leatherback has a leathery and slightly flexible shell. The top of the shell is called the carapace. The plates of the carapace are called scutes. The bottom of the shell is the plastron.

[Despite what is sometimes shown in cartoons, a turtle cannot actually get out of its shell. A turtle's shell is attached to its spine and to the rest of its skeleton.]

◄ THE PLATES THAT MAKE UP THE CARAPACE, OR THE TOP OF THE SHELL, ARE CALLED SCUTES.

Marine Turtles Are Adapted for Life at Sea

Turtle Adaptations

1. The front and hind limbs of marine turtles are flattened flippers for swimming.
2. The front flippers power the turtle's swimming.
3. The rear flippers are used for steering.

▼ MARINE TURTLES ARE POWERFUL SWIMMERS.

▲ TURTLE EYES ARE ADAPTED TO SEE WELL
UNDERWATER.

4. Life in the ocean means that marine turtles
   take in a lot of salt. Marine turtles get rid of
   this extra salt through salty tears, which are
   shed through a special gland near the eyes.
5. Turtles can see quite well underwater, but they
   cannot see very far on land.

[All marine turtles' flippers are not the same. Hawksbill
turtles have two claws on their flippers, but green turtles
have only one claw. Leatherback turtles have no claws on
their flippers.]

Marine Turtles Can Grow Very Large

The leatherback is the largest of all turtles. Adults can reach 6 feet (1.8 meters) in length and weigh about 1,100 pounds (500 kilograms).

The green turtle is smaller than the leatherback but larger than all the other marine turtles. Mature green turtles measure about 3 feet (1 meter) in length and usually weigh 200 to 400 pounds (90 to 180 kilograms).

The hawksbill can weigh more than some adult humans but is small compared to other turtle species. Mature hawksbills are approximately 35 inches (90 centimeters) long and weigh up to 160 pounds (70 kilograms).

► RESEARCHERS MEASURE A LEATHERBACK TURTLE.

REASON TO CARE # 7

Marine Turtle Populations Are Declining

Before modern times, coastal people around the world hunted turtles without a huge impact on turtle populations. Later, European exploration and settlement began a time of widespread turtle consumption. As global trade developed, humans sold turtles and turtle eggs in large quantities for food. Hawksbills were sold for their beautiful shells, which were used in art and jewelry. Coastal development began to carve away at turtles' nesting habitats, and commercial fishing devastated the remaining global turtle populations.

In 1982, marine turtles were internationally recognized as endangered by the International Union for the Conservation of Nature (IUCN) when they were added to the IUCN Red List of Threatened Species. Although green turtles are considered to be slightly less endangered than hawksbill or leatherback turtles, all three species are quickly declining.

◀ TURTLES ARE STILL KILLED AND SOLD FOR FOOD IN SOME AREAS OF THE WORLD.

There Is Hope for Marine Turtles

Today, some populations of marine turtles are holding steady. Thanks to the efforts of many people, organizations, and governments, some turtle populations are growing. The global turtle population, however, is still at great risk of extinction. If overall current trends continue, marine turtles may become extinct in the next decades. But there is certainly still hope. Global collaboration on widespread conservation efforts could give turtles another chance for survival.

[For thousands of years, turtles and turtle eggs have been important foods for many seaside human populations. As turtles disappear, so does this traditional food source. Many seaside communities are working to protect local turtle populations.]

► THESE CHILDREN IN THE PHILIPPINES ARE RELEASING BABY TURTLES AS PART OF A LOCAL CONSERVATION EFFORT.

TYPES OF MARINE TURTLES

REASON TO CARE # 9

The Leatherback Turtle Is Unique

The leatherback's carapace is unlike all the other sea turtles. Its smooth shell has no scutes. Instead, it has seven ridges that run from head to tail. Its shell is softer and more flexible than other turtles' shells. Leatherbacks are speckled black and pinkish-white.

The leatherback population has declined sharply during recent decades. In just one generation, the total number of leatherbacks is believed to have dropped about 80 percent.

[The leatherback sets records. It is the largest sea turtle and the fastest swimmer. It travels the longest distances and swims in the coldest seas. The leatherback also dives deeper than any other reptile. One turtle was measured diving 4,035 feet below the surface.]

◄ TOP: NEWLY HATCHED LEATHERBACK TURTLES. BOTTOM: LEATHERBACK TURTLES DIVE DEEP UNDERWATER.

The Leatherback Lives Far from Land

Leatherbacks spend most of their time in the open ocean, far from land. Females come to shore only to nest on sandy tropical beaches. Males rarely, if ever, swim near shore. The leatherback has the greatest range of any marine turtle and may swim thousands of miles through the ocean. They tolerate colder waters than other sea turtles and may be found in waters as cold as 30 to 40 degrees Fahrenheit. Unlike most reptiles, leatherbacks can maintain a higher body temperature than the surrounding air or water.

▼ LEATHERBACK TURTLES ONLY LEAVE THE WATER TO LAY EGGS.

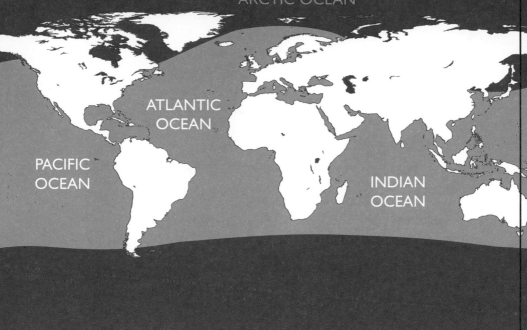

▲ LEATHERBACKS SWIM IN EVERY OCEAN ON EARTH.

Leatherback turtles roam in every ocean in the world. They build nests in tropical and subtropical areas on the coasts of North America, South America, Africa, Asia, and Australia, and on many islands in the Pacific Ocean.

Green Turtles Are Not Green

The green turtle is not actually green. Its carapace is patterned with browns and olive colors, and its plastron is a lighter yellowish white. It gets its name from the green-colored fat under its shell.

Males and females can be distinguished by the lengths of their tails. Males have longer tails that stick out beyond the carapace. Females have tails that barely reach the end of the carapace.

[Green turtles swim great distances quickly. They can travel up to 300 miles in ten days.]

▶ A GREEN TURTLE IS ACTUALLY BROWN.

Green Turtles Live in the Tropics

Green turtles live in tropical and subtropical waters all over the world. They migrate between nesting and feeding grounds, mostly staying close to shore where their main foods—sea grass and algae—grow. An important nesting site for green turtles in the United States is at the French Frigate Shoals in Hawaii.

▼ GREEN TURTLES MOSTLY EAT SEA GRASSES AND ALGAE.

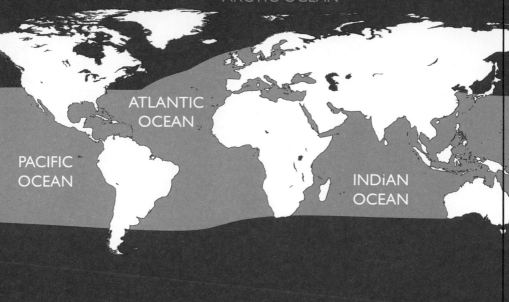

ARCTIC OCEAN

ATLANTIC
OCEAN

PACIFIC
OCEAN

INDiAN
OCEAN

▲ GREEN TURTLES MIGRATE ALL OVER THE WORLD,
STAYING IN WARMER WATERS.

[Like other marine turtles, green turtles are known to migrate
great distances. One population of green turtles that feeds in
Brazil nests on Ascension Island in the middle of the Atlantic
Ocean, more than 1,200 miles away.]

REASON TO CARE # 13
The Hawksbill Has a Pointed Beak

The hawksbill turtle's carapace is golden yellow, brown, and black. Its plastron is amber or clear yellow. Near its tail, the hawksbill's carapace is jagged, with pointy overlapping scutes. The hawksbill is named for its beak, which is pointed and curved, almost like a hawk's. Male hawksbill turtles have thicker tails than females.

[Some people consider the hawksbill to be the prettiest turtle. Unfortunately, the hawksbill's beauty puts it at greater risk for poaching.]

◄ A HAWKSBILL'S BEAK HELPS IT EAT CORAL AND SPONGES.

Hawksbills Live Near Tropical Reefs

Hawksbills live in warm, tropical waters near coral reefs and nest on tropical beaches all over the world. Like other marine turtles, they migrate between feeding grounds and the beaches where they nest. They play an important role in the reef ecosystem and food web. As predators of marine sponges, hawksbills help to keep the sponge population under control. Without these important predators, sponge populations could get overgrown and threaten other reef organisms.

▼ HAWKSBILLS LIVE NEAR CORAL REEFS.

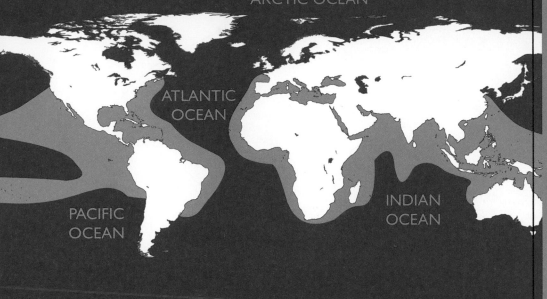

ARCTIC OCEAN

ATLANTIC
OCEAN

PACIFIC
OCEAN

INDIAN
OCEAN

▲ HAWKSBILL TURTLES LIVE IN TROPICAL WATERS.

[Reefs are home to thousands of species of underwater life,
including plants, fish, clams, snails, urchins, sponges, starfish, and
many varieties of coral.]

MARINE TURTLE LIFE

REASON TO CARE # 15

Marine Turtles Eat Different Foods

Different kinds of turtles have different diets. Hawksbills are omnivores. They mostly eat sponges and other coral reef organisms, but they may also eat some algae. Leatherbacks are carnivores. They eat jellyfish and other soft-bodied animals that live in the open ocean. Young green turtles are omnivores. They eat plants, crabs, jellyfish, and other small sea creatures. However, adult green turtles are mostly herbivores. They eat algae and sea grass almost exclusively.

[A carnivore eats only animals. An omnivore eats both plants and animals. An herbivore eats only plants.]

◀ TOP: A GREEN SEA TURTLE EATS SEA GRASS. BOTTOM: A JELLYFISH FLOATS IN THE OCEAN.

Marine Turtles Have Adaptations for Eating

Each species of marine turtle has special adaptations for capturing and eating food. Leatherbacks, for example, have spines in their throats that help trap their slippery prey. Sharp edges on green turtles' beaks help to cut through the sea grasses, and bacteria in their intestines helps digest their vegetable diet. The hawksbill's pointed beak lets it get in between tight spaces in coral reefs, where it feeds.

▼ HAWKSBILLS USE THEIR POINTED BEAKS TO GET FOOD FROM TIGHT SPACES.

▲ A GREEN TURTLE'S SHARP BEAK EASILY CUTS THE SEA GRASSES IT EATS.

[Many organisms are injured by the jellyfish's sting—but not the leatherback. The leatherback is one of the few organisms that eats jellyfish. Few creatures can handle the toxins in sponges—except the hawksbill turtle. Both of these marine turtles have adapted to eat organisms that few other animals can consume.]

Marine Turtles Are Part of Ocean Food Webs

Hawksbills are an important part of the coral reef ecosystem. Hawksbills keep sponge populations from taking over the reef, helping to balance the populations of different reef organisms. Coral reef ecosystems are at risk, due in part to climate change. Just as coral reefs depend on hawksbills, hawksbills depend on coral reefs.

Adult green turtles are also important in their own ecosystem near the shore, where they eat sea grass. These ocean ecosystems must be preserved to ensure that marine turtles will have food to eat.

[One acre of sea grass habitat can be home to forty thousand fish and 50 million smaller sea creatures such as clams and crabs.]

► CORAL REEF FOOD WEBS DEPEND ON HAWKSBILL TURTLES.

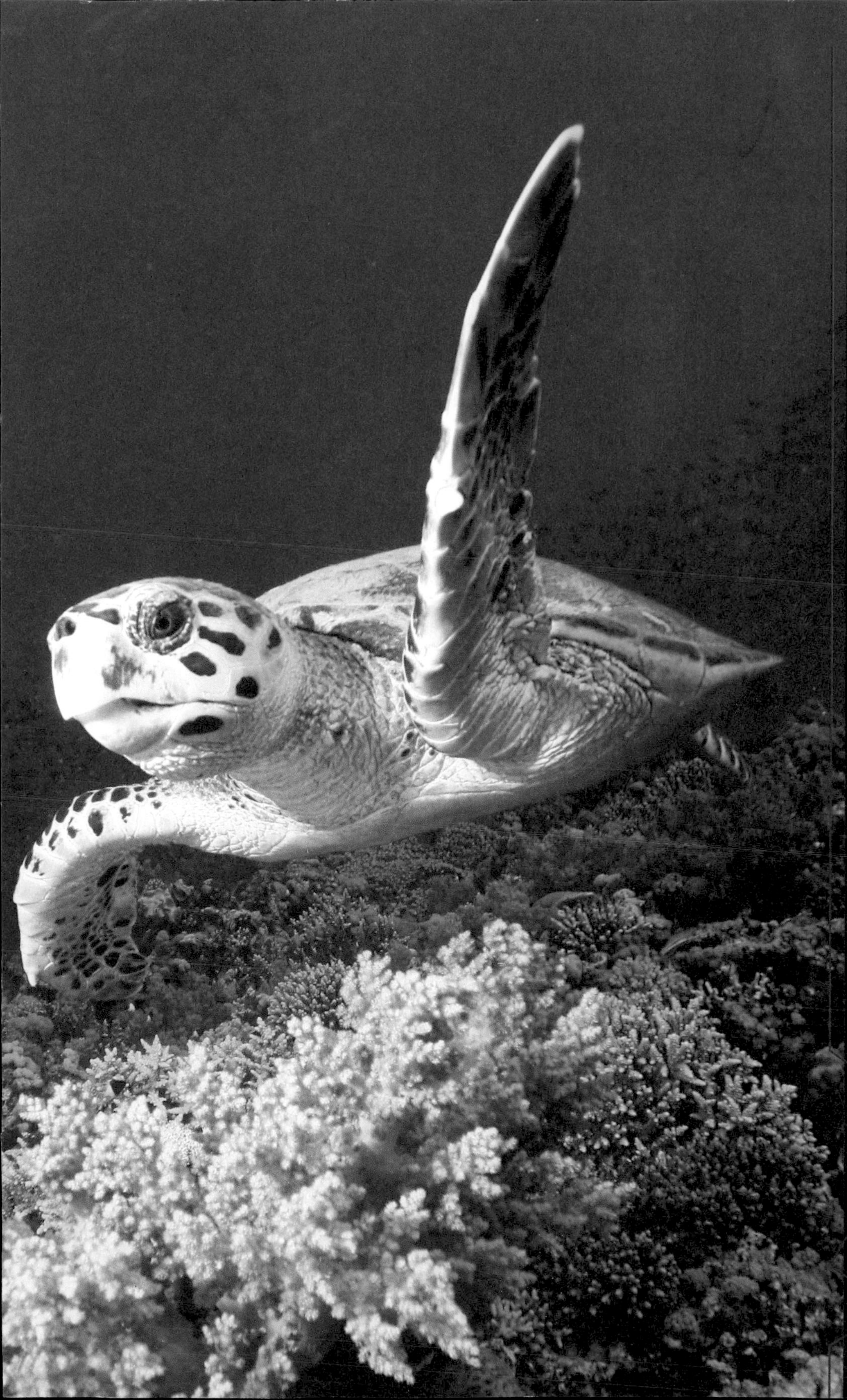

REASON TO CARE # 18

Marine Turtles
Have Predators

Marine turtle eggs are particularly vulnerable to predators such as raccoons, dogs, and other mammals. Baby turtles are in danger, too. As they scramble to sea, they might turn into a meal for a ghost crab or a yellow night heron. In the ocean, while they are still small, they might be eaten by birds or fish. Sharks also attack adult sea turtles, but turtle shells are good protection. Sometimes a shark will only bite part of a flipper.

Once they reach maturity, however, marine turtles' main causes of death are due to humans and old age. Humans are the main predators of marine turtles. Most scientists agree that the best way to conserve marine turtles is to reduce the risk of death for the largest and oldest females in the population.

◄ SHARKS ARE ONE OF THE MARINE TURTLES' PREDATORS.

Fish and Shrimp Keep Marine Turtles Clean

Over time, barnacles, algae, and other organisms build up on marine turtles' shells. Too many barnacles can slow a turtle down. Turtles are known to stop at "cleaning stations," where other sea organisms, such as fish and shrimp, pick the turtles' shells clean. This type of relationship, in which both sides benefit, is called mutualism. The fish and shrimp get a meal, and the turtles get clean shells. Other marine animals also appreciate the "cleaning service."

Barber pole shrimps have been observed cleaning hawksbill turtles on the coast of northeastern Brazil. Fish called wrasses clean green turtles in Hawaii and in other locations.

▶ A SCHOOL OF SURGEONFISH CLEANS THIS GREEN TURTLE.

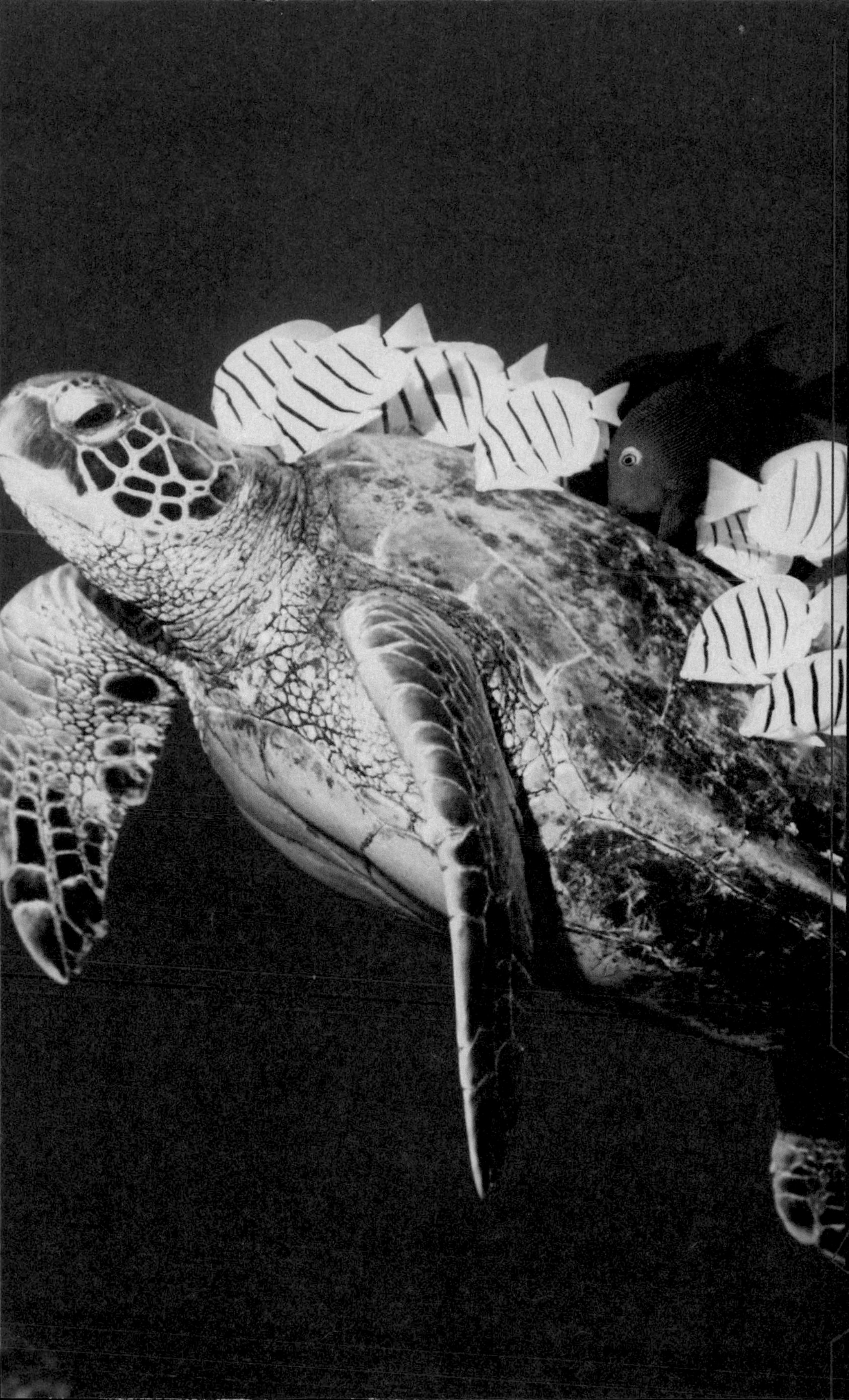

REASON TO CARE # 20

Marine Turtles Move on Land and at Sea

Sea turtles use their powerful front flippers to propel themselves through the water. Some marine turtles can swim as fast as 30 miles per hour for short distances. On land, their flippers are not quite as graceful. As they flap their flippers back and forth, sea turtles slowly move themselves over the sand. The size and shape of the tracks left on the beach are slightly different for each species.

[Almost all marine turtle tracks are left by females. Male turtles rarely return to land after they hatch.]

◄ TURTLES SWIM GRACEFULLY.

REASON TO CARE # 21

Marine Turtles
Have No Ears

Turtles do not really have ears—at least not external ears. Turtles can, however, hear sound through internal ear structures. They can hear the low frequency sounds typical of an underwater environment. Turtles can see much better underwater than they can on land. It may be hard to imagine, but turtles can also smell underwater. Marine turtles do not have vocal cords and do not make much noise. Their breathing, however, may make raspy or grunt-like sounds.

[Various studies have suggested that some marine turtles may use bubbles, sounds, or odors to find mates.]

◄ TURTLES HAVE NO EXTERNAL EARS, BUT THEY CAN HEAR WITH INTERNAL EAR STRUCTURES.

Marine Turtles
Use Body Language

Marine turtles use body language to communicate certain messages. If a turtle feels threatened, it might open its mouth wide or move its head up and down. If the turtle is particularly upset, it might swipe its flipper up toward its head. This means back off! Researchers and snorkelers might see these turtle signals if they get too close.

▼ A TURTLE'S BODY LANGUAGE TELLS WHEN IT IS UPSET.

▲ TURTLES RETURN TO NEST ON THE SAME BEACH
WHERE THEY WERE BORN.

REASON TO CARE # 23

Marine Turtles Use Magnetic Maps

A magnet has two ends, or poles. Earth is like a giant magnet, with two magnetic poles—North and South. Marine turtles are thought to use Earth's magnetic information to navigate the ocean. Scientists continue to study how marine turtles and other organisms use magnetic maps. Even after a decade or more has passed, marine turtles somehow manage to return to the beaches where they were born.

YOUNG MARINE TURTLES

> REASON TO CARE # 24
>
> ## Marine Turtles Build Beachfront Nests

Under nighttime skies, female turtles come ashore to build their nests. Their flippers, so elegant for swimming, are awkward on land. A turtle flops her way up the shore and then settles in to dig. She must get above the high tide line, or else her nest will drown.

First, she uses her front flippers to hollow out a large shallow hole that she can nestle into. Then, using her rear flippers, she digs a deeper hole in which she will lay the eggs. Once filled with eggs, the mother turtle fills the hole with sand and brushes sand over the entire area, disguising the nest.

[Turtles shed salty "tears" from glands near their eyes. This makes nesting females look like they are crying—but these tears have nothing to do with sadness. The tears help get rid of extra salt in the turtles' bodies.]

◀ TURTLES DIG DEEP HOLES IN ORDER TO HIDE THEIR EGGS.

Marine Turtles Do Not Nest Every Year

Nesting occurs at different times in different parts of the world, but it usually occurs during warm months. Marine turtles return to shore to nest every few years. When nesting occurs, a female can lay several clutches, or sets, of eggs. Between laying each clutch, the female returns to the ocean, spending around ten days in the water.

▼ TURTLES RETURN TO THE OCEAN BETWEEN LAYING EACH SET OF EGGS.

▲ A GREEN TURTLE LAYS HER EGGS.

REASON TO CARE # 26

Marine Turtle Eggs Are Soft

Unlike bird eggs, turtle eggs are round and have a soft shell. The soft shell means the eggs do not break as they tumble down into the nest, piling on top of one another. A female turtle can lay about fifty to one hundred eggs at a time. Most sea turtle eggs are about the size of a ping-pong ball. The eggs of the leatherback are slightly larger.

Egg Temperature Is Important

The temperature at which an egg incubates determines the sex of the baby turtle inside. Females hatch from eggs that incubate at higher temperatures, and males hatch from eggs that incubate at lower temperatures. The eggs at the center of the nest tend to be warmer than the eggs at the edges. However, if a year is particularly warm or cool, it may affect the temperature of the entire nest. In these cases, all of the hatchlings may be female or all may be male.

[For green turtles, a temperature of 82 degrees Fahrenheit will produce males. At a temperature of 88 degrees Fahrenheit, the eggs will hatch as females.]

▶ THESE EGGS WILL HATCH LEATHERBACK TURTLES.

A Baby's Egg Tooth Breaks Its Shell

After about two months of development, it is time for a sea turtle egg to hatch. A baby turtle has a pointed little structure on the end of its beak called an egg tooth. The turtle uses this tooth to break out of the shell. Then, the tiny turtle scrambles around in the sand, slowly making its way up to the surface of the beach. It can take several days for a hatchling to reach the surface. Eventually, a baby turtle's egg tooth falls off.

▼ BABY MARINE TURTLES ARE TINY.

▲ GREEN TURTLES EMERGE FROM THEIR NEST IN SRI LANKA.

[A baby green turtle is about 2 inches (5 centimeters) long and weighs less than 1 ounce (28 grams).]

REASON TO CARE # 29

Baby Turtles Take a Dangerous Route

Baby turtles may have to travel dozens of feet from their nest to the ocean. For a 2-inch (5-centimeter) hatchling, this is a long journey— and a risky one. Along the way, many baby turtles will be eaten by predators. Once they reach the water, they are still at risk from ocean predators.

Of the hatchlings that reach the ocean, only a few will survive. Scientists estimate that as few as one in one thousand baby turtles will reach maturity. After ten to thirty years at sea, surviving turtles find their way back to nest on the same beach where they were born, and the cycle of life continues.

[Some predators of eggs and baby turtles include birds, crabs, fish, and mammals such as raccoons, dogs, and foxes.]

◄ A HOOD ISLAND MOCKINGBIRD CATCHES A TURTLE HATCHLING.

Baby Turtles Follow the Light to the Sea

Once they emerge from the nest, how do baby turtles know which way to crawl? Many scientists believe that they aim for the light. Reflected by the water, the sky is lighter over the ocean than over the land—even at night.

Streetlamps and other lights near the shore can confuse baby turtles, sending them in the wrong direction. Many seaside populations have rules to limit lighting during turtle nesting season.

[Marine turtle hatchlings often wait until after dark to leave their nests. They usually head for the water in groups. Both of these habits help the hatchlings increase their chances of reaching the ocean.]

▶ HATCHLING TURTLES FOLLOW THE LIGHT TO THE SEA.

REASON TO CARE # 31

Young Marine Turtles Get Lost

Once baby turtles reach the sea, they are hard to follow. They disappear into the ocean and may not be seen again for several years. This time period is commonly called the "lost years."

Scientists have pieced together a probable theory for the young years of green turtles and hawksbills. Green turtles spend the first few years of their lives in the open ocean. As adults, they spend most of their time near the coast where they can feed on sea grass.

Hawksbill turtles are thought to spend several years in the open ocean, feeding on floating vegetation. As larger juveniles and as adults, they live near coral reefs.

Scientists have not successfully studied the habitat and behaviors of young leatherbacks. Young leatherbacks remain a mystery.

◀ THIS GREEN TURTLE HATCHLING HEADS OUT TO SEA, WHERE IT WILL REMAIN FOR SEVERAL YEARS.

Marine Turtles Must Migrate

Both male and female turtles migrate between feeding grounds and nesting grounds, but only the females come ashore. The turtles mate in the waters near the nesting grounds. A turtle's migration can be very long. Feeding grounds and nesting grounds are often hundreds or thousands of miles apart. Leatherbacks are known to travel the farthest—more than 3,000 miles, which is greater than the distance from Los Angeles, California, to New York, New York. Most turtles return to the same beaches where they were born to lay their own eggs.

► TURTLES MIGRATE GREAT DISTANCES FROM THEIR FEEDING GROUNDS TO THEIR NESTING GROUNDS.

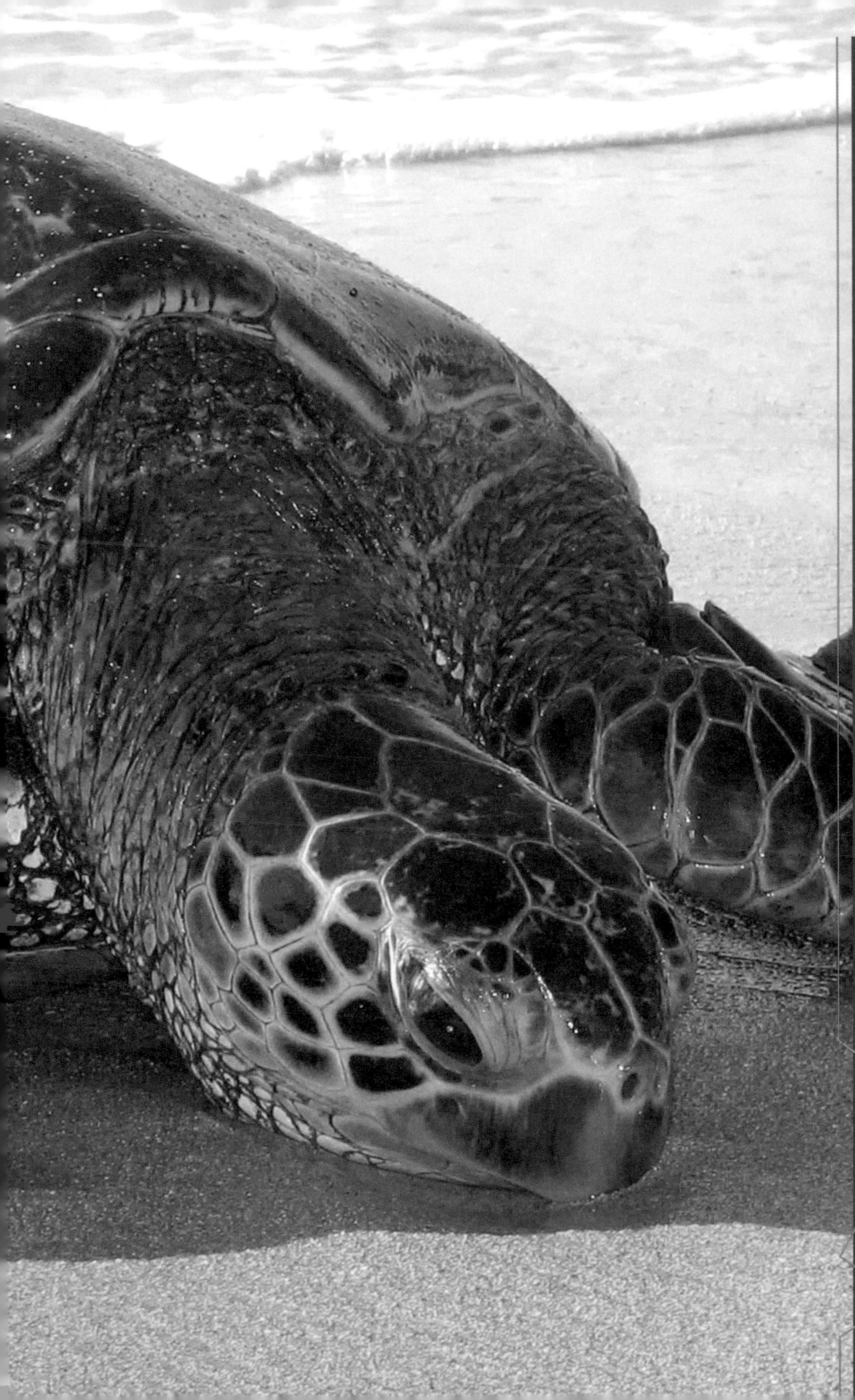

MARINE TURTLES IN CULTURE

REASON TO CARE # 33

The Marine Turtle Is a Spiritual Symbol

The turtle is a spiritual symbol in many traditions. According to the traditional stories of the Arapaho people of the western United States, the world started with only water and no land. A turtle, accompanied by a person, dove down into the water and returned with a piece of earth, creating the land. For the Ngöbe-Buglé people in Panama, who live near nesting populations of turtles at Chiriquí Beach, the leatherback is a symbol of life and rebirth.

◄ ACCORDING TO THE HINDU CREATION STORY, TURTLES WERE PRESENT AT THE CREATION OF THE WORLD, AS DEPICTED AT THE TEMPLE OF ANGKOR WAT.

Marine Turtles
Inspired Legends

According to an ancient Fijian legend, some turtles were once humans. A long time ago, two women were captured by fishermen from an enemy village. The women were trapped in the men's boat. The women managed to escape by turning into turtles and swimming back to shore. Legend tells that the women stayed turtles, and their descendants are the turtles that live in the area today.

In the Fijian village of Namuana, "turtle calling" is a traditional practice. Before calling for the turtles, people gather to tell this legend of the humans that became turtles. Then, through music, song, and dance, women call for the turtles to surface in the ocean. Some people believe the turtles will not come if anyone from the enemy village is nearby.

▶ SOME PEOPLE BELIEVE A TRADITIONAL FIJIAN SONG CAN CALL TURTLES TO THE OCEAN'S SURFACE.

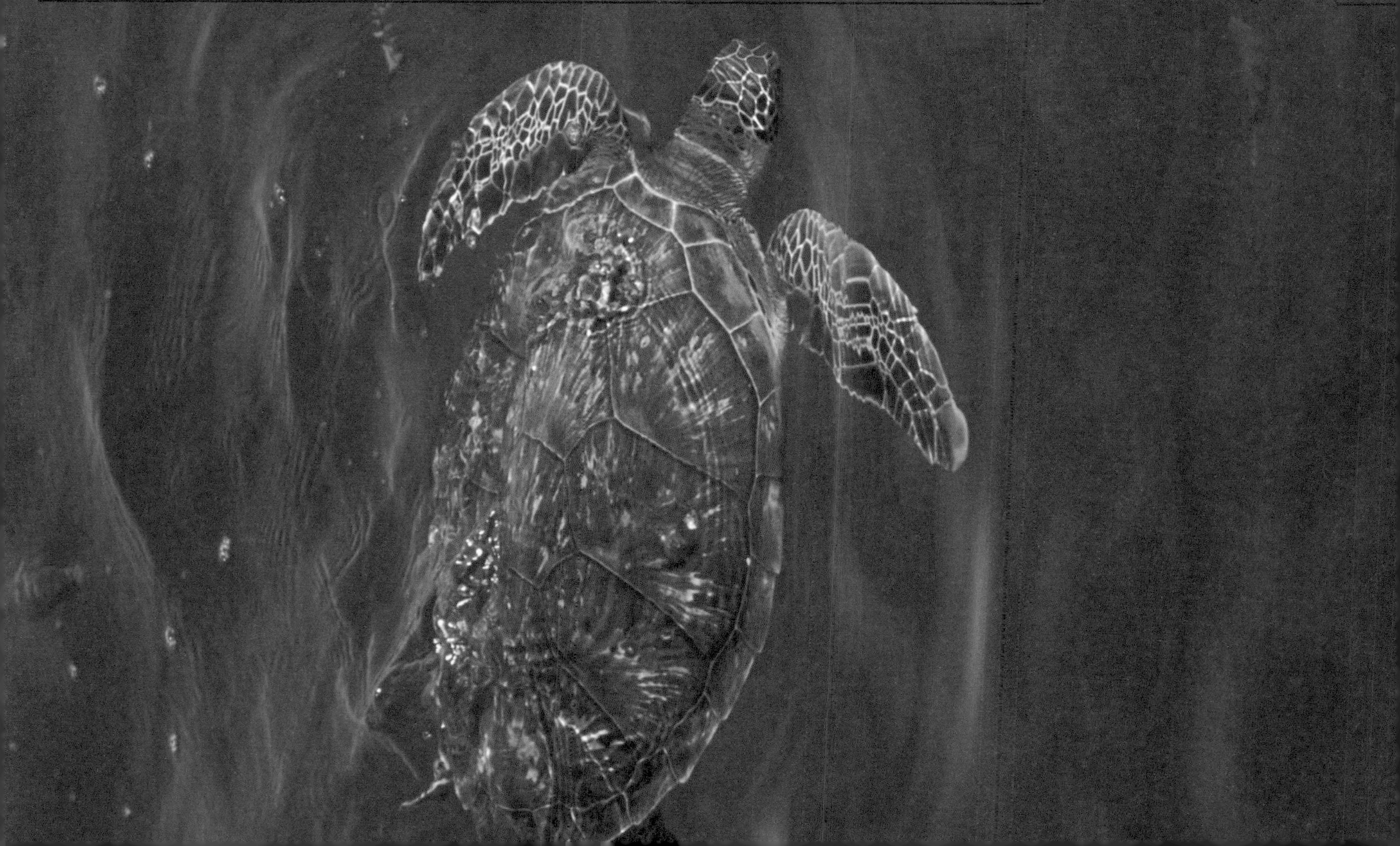

A Legendary Turtle Protects Children

A Hawaiian legend tells the story of a special turtle named Kauila, who could turn into a human girl. Kauila was born on the shores of Punalu'u. As protector of children, she watched over them as they played along the shore and sometimes joined in the fun. According to the legend, Kauila's parents dug a deep hole that became a freshwater spring. Kauila was the guardian of the spring, which provided drinking water for the village people.

[Kauila's home, Punalu'u, is a black sand beach on Hawaii's Big Island.]

▶ A GREEN TURTLE COMES ASHORE ON A BLACK SAND BEACH IN HAWAII.

REASON TO CARE # 36

Marine Turtles Are Used in Ceremonies

Turtles play important roles in the ceremonies of many cultures. On Taiwan's Penghu Islands, sea turtles are symbols of good luck and long life. During the Lantern Festival, two weeks after Chinese New Year, Penghu islanders sacrifice turtles—but not real ones. Most of the turtles used in the Lantern Festival are turtle-shaped rice cakes. Other sacrificial turtles may be made out of bags of rice flour, coins, or even gold. These turtle representations are placed in temples as sacrifices to the gods.

[The turtle is the Chinese symbol for longevity and wisdom. Sometimes, its shell represents the universe. The flat bottom shell is the earth and the rounded top is the sky.]

◄ THIS TURTLE STATUE GUARDS A CHINESE BUILDING.

Turtle Shells Are Used in Art

Humans have crafted accessories and jewelry out of hawksbill turtle shells for thousands of years. This tradition is called *bekko* in Japanese. Turtle shell accessories have also been popular in other parts of the world. Combs and eyeglass frames made from hawksbill shells were in high demand in Europe and North America in the 1800s and 1900s.

▼ A PRESERVED TURTLE FOR SALE IN A SHOP IN SINGAPORE

Today, the commercial import or export of hawksbill shells is illegal. However, bekko artists still may make crafts using shells stockpiled from years past. In the future, this art form can continue only if hawksbill turtle populations thrive.

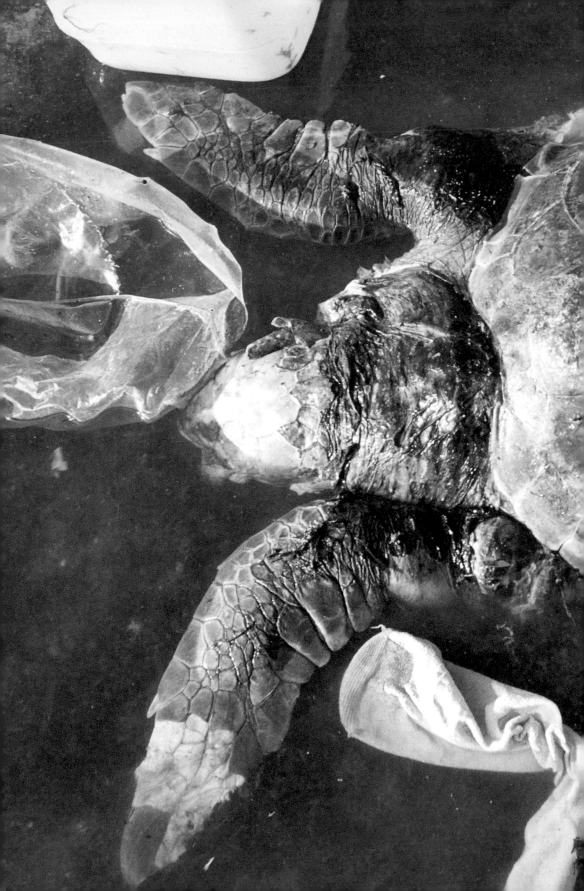

REASON TO CARE # 38

Human Activity Threatens Marine Turtles

Nearly all threats to marine turtle populations are the result of human activity. Many turtles are killed unintentionally by commercial fishing equipment. Turtles can drown when tangled in fishing lines and nets. Pollution is another main threat. Leatherbacks sometimes mistake plastic bags for jellyfish and choke while swallowing.

Some turtles and turtle eggs are hunted for food. Limited hunting might be sustainable with a thriving turtle population, but with global population declines, hunting is a threat. Building on and near beaches can interfere with nesting.

[Conservation groups are concerned that offshore oil drilling threatens turtles. The building of oil rigs can damage marine habitats and coastlines. Oil spills can devastate an ecosystem, and even small amounts of oil are toxic to turtles.]

◀ POLLUTION IS A BIG THREAT TO TURTLES.

Climate Change Affects Coral Reefs

Climate change affects ocean ecosystems, including coral reefs. Climate change raises ocean temperatures. Rising carbon dioxide levels affect ocean chemistry by changing the levels of acid in the water. Changing acid levels make survival difficult for the tiny animals that make up coral reefs. Over the last few decades, these factors, in combination with other disturbances, have resulted in a global decline in coral reef communities.

Coral reefs are home to many organisms, including hawksbills. Hawksbills depend on coral reefs for food. Dying reefs may therefore directly threaten these turtles. Of course, climate change impacts all marine turtles.

[Some of the color of coral reefs comes from algae. Algae are tiny plants that live in water. Temperature changes can kill the algae, resulting in a phenomenon called coral bleaching.]

▶ THIS CORAL REEF HAS BEEN BLEACHED.

REASON TO CARE # 40

Green Turtles Are Threatened by Disease

Fibropapillomatosis (feye-broh-pap-il-oh-mah-TOH-siss) is a disease that threatens green turtle populations in Florida and in other locations. This disease causes tumors to grow on a turtle's body. Tumors on the head can cause blindness or make it hard for a turtle to eat. Tumors can also grow inside the turtle, interfering with the turtle's lungs, heart, or other organs. The tumors themselves are not harmful, but if they disrupt a turtle's regular body functions and behavior, they can eventually cause death.

The disease was first identified in the 1930s. In recent decades, the number of turtles affected has increased dramatically. Although most common in green turtles, it can also affect other marine turtles. Scientists continue to work to understand more about the causes of this disease and how it is transmitted.

◀ RESEARCHERS NAMED THIS GREEN TURTLE AKEBONO. HE WAS LAST SEEN IN 2003 AND HAS PROBABLY DIED.

Shrimp Trawling Can Catch Marine Turtles

Shrimp trawling is a fishing method used to catch shrimp. A large net is dragged across the ocean, scooping up everything in its path. In recent decades, shrimp trawling has caused the deaths of many marine animals, including turtles. Today, shrimp trawlers in many countries use nets that have a turtle excluder device. This allows marine animals to escape if they are swept up in the net.

▼ A TURTLE ESCAPES FROM A NET THROUGH A TURTLE EXCLUDER DEVICE.

▲ THIS MARINE TURTLE WAS CAUGHT FOR FOOD IN INDONESIA.

REASON TO CARE # 42

Marine Turtles Can Be Poisonous

In some impoverished coastal communities, people still eat turtles to survive. Turtle meat can contain disease-causing bacteria, high levels of pollutants, and other toxins. Sometimes people are poisoned by turtle meat and become very ill or even die. Education and public health efforts could help increase awareness of the risks of turtle consumption. These programs could also help communities find alternative food sources. By reducing turtle consumption, human lives might be saved along with the turtles.

Marine Turtles Do Not Thrive in Captivity

As protected species, marine turtles cannot be held in captivity without a permit. Some turtles are raised in captivity, with permission, for research and education. Turtles that have suffered severe injuries and might not survive in the wild may find a home in an aquarium.

Leatherbacks do not survive very long in captivity. A leatherback in a tank will constantly try to dive down and swim forward—even if it has reached the end of the tank. As a result, it can injure itself by repeatedly hitting the glass.

A researcher at the University of British Columbia recently developed one way to avoid this problem. T. Todd Jones came up with the idea of putting a leatherback into a rubbery harness—almost like a bouncy seat for a toddler. The harness holds the turtle in place, even as it swims and dives in the tank.

[Although it has been proven possible to breed some types of marine turtles in captivity, most experiments have failed. Breeding marine turtles remains very difficult and expensive.]

▶ THIS GREEN TURTLE LIVES IN AN AQUARIUM IN THE BAHAMAS.

REASON TO CARE # 44

Baseline Numbers Set Goals for Recovery

A baseline is the normal or expected size of a population—how many turtles there should be. A baseline number allows scientists to judge how endangered a species is. Scientists warn that we need to think carefully about baseline values— that is, what numbers are normal—for marine turtle populations.

Baseline values should account for how many marine turtles there were in the past, not just recent numbers. However, we almost never have exact counts for historical populations, so it is difficult to determine an accurate baseline. Still, a baseline value is important because it can help set goals for population recovery.

[Some scientists have estimated that the population of green turtles in the Caribbean has declined up to 99 percent since Christopher Columbus visited the islands in the 1490s.]

◀ IT IS DIFFICULT TO ESTIMATE HOW MANY TURTLES MAKE A HEALTHY POPULATION.

Scientists Track Marine Turtles

Tracking the movement of sea turtles gives important information about where sea turtles feed and nest, how far they travel, how fast they grow, and how long they live. For decades, scientists have tagged turtles' flippers with plastic or metal tags. Each tag has a unique code of numbers and letters. Once tagged, turtles are released. Then, if a tagged turtle is found again, it can be identified. However, most tagged turtles are never seen again.

[Turtle researchers keep a master list on the Internet of all the turtles that have ever been tagged. This way, if a turtle is found again, all of the information about it is kept in one place.]

▶ THIS GREEN TURTLE HAS A TAG ON ITS RIGHT FRONT FLIPPER.

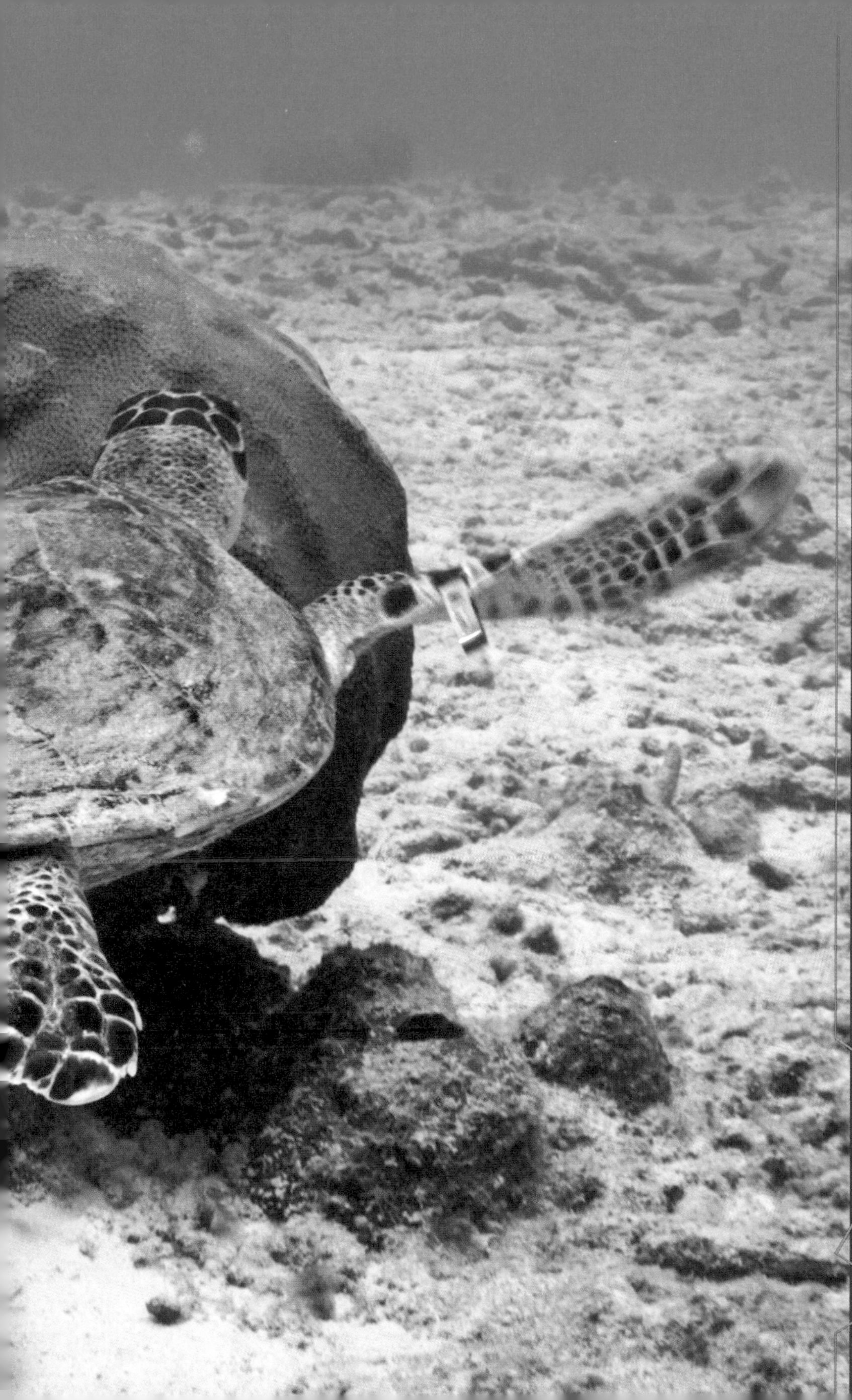

REASON TO CARE # 46

Satellites Track Marine Turtles

With satellite tags, turtles can be tracked continuously—not just when they happen to be seen on shore. Satellite tracking allows researchers—and the public—to track the real-time movement of sea turtles around the globe. Regularly updated maps of many tagged turtles can be accessed on the Internet. Turtles are tracked using the same satellites that make GPS (Global Positioning System) possible.

[A turtle called Jamur was tagged in Panama. Satellite tracking showed that it traveled almost 7,500 miles in one year!]

◄ THIS LEATHERBACK TURTLE WAS JUST FITTED WITH A SATELLITE DEVICE TO TRACK ITS MOVEMENTS.

Marine Turtles Get a Head Start

One method of turtle conservation is known as "head starting." Scientists or conservation groups identify turtle nests that are at risk and take steps to preserve them. This might include putting a fence around the threatened nest or even moving it. When the turtles hatch, scientists catch them and raise them in captivity for nine months to a year. When the turtles are bigger, they are released into the wild. The hope is that these larger turtles are less at risk of dying or being eaten than newly hatched turtles.

However, some people are concerned that turtles that have been head started are not normal. Although some of these turtles seem to lead normal lives after their release, others move and migrate in strange ways. Some do not mate or lay eggs as they should. Critics of head starting believe that these turtles cannot live normally because they did not migrate in their first year of life. More research is needed to determine if head-started turtles can lead normal lives.

▶ A SCIENTIST EXAMINES BABY TURTLES TO DECIDE IF THEY CAN BE RELEASED SOON.

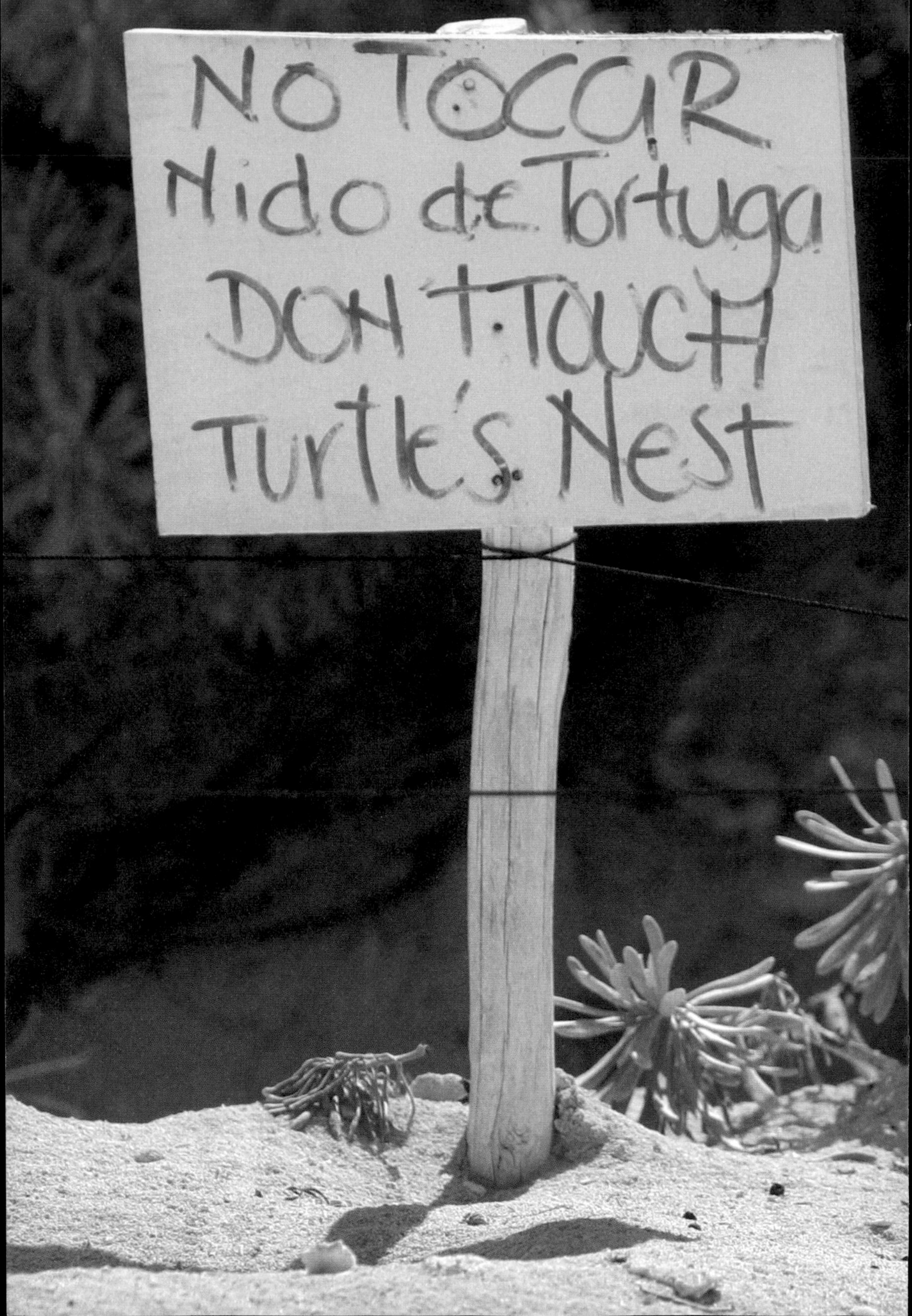
NO TOCAR
Nido de Tortuga
DON'T TOUCH
Turtle's Nest

REASON TO CARE # 48

Some Marine Turtles Are Making a Comeback

Although sea turtles remain at risk today, many success stories offer hope for their future. Collaborative conservation efforts in Tortuguero, Costa Rica, have resulted in a growing count of green turtle nests—now numbering more than one hundred thousand. At Panama's Chiriquí Beach, a leatherback population more than 4,500 turtles strong is thriving under the care of local citizens, who have collaborated with international conservation groups. With international efforts, these numbers could continue to grow.

[Most places in the world where marine turtles are found have conservation groups run by local citizens. The work of these groups is critical for saving marine turtles.]

◄ A SIGN WARNS PASSERSBY NOT TO DISTURB THE NEST OF AN ENDANGERED MARINE TURTLE.

Conservation Groups Protect Turtles

Marine turtles are international citizens, swimming the seas and nesting on the shores of hundreds of different countries. Global turtle preservation requires that many governments work together toward a common goal. Many programs around the world are taking important steps toward protecting marine turtles. One successful conservation program, called TAMAR, has been in operation in Brazil for about three decades. Now, TAMAR is working with Uruguay and Argentina to expand its impact. Successful conservation efforts occur through the collaboration of governments, organizations, and local citizens.

► LOCAL CITIZENS WORK WITH A CONSERVATION GROUP IN INDONESIA.

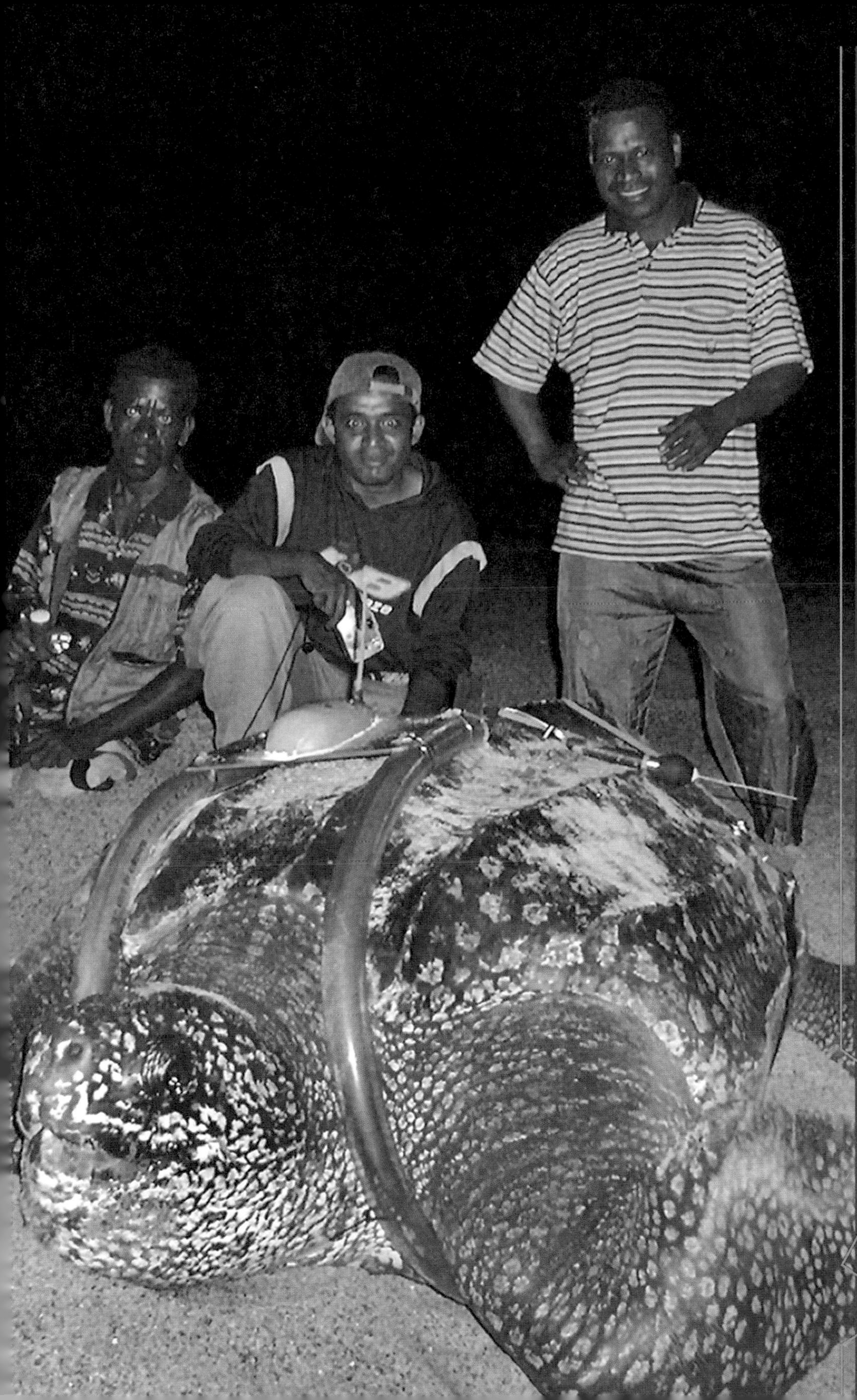

You Can Help Save Marine Turtles

Fun and Rewarding Ways to Help Save Marine Turtles

- Read books and newspaper articles about turtles.
- Visit aquariums that have turtles so you can see them up close.
- Keep informed. Read updates on turtle populations on the Internet. See the Internet Addresses section in the back of this book for suggestions.
- If you live or travel somewhere turtle products are sold, do not buy these products.
- If you live near a shoreline where turtles nest, consider joining a local organization that helps protect the turtles' shoreline habitat.
- Use cloth bags and reusable containers when possible. Throwing out plastic can add to ocean pollution.
- Only purchase and eat seafood that is caught according to the best environmental practices.
- Have your class plan a fund-raiser to support a turtle conservation group.

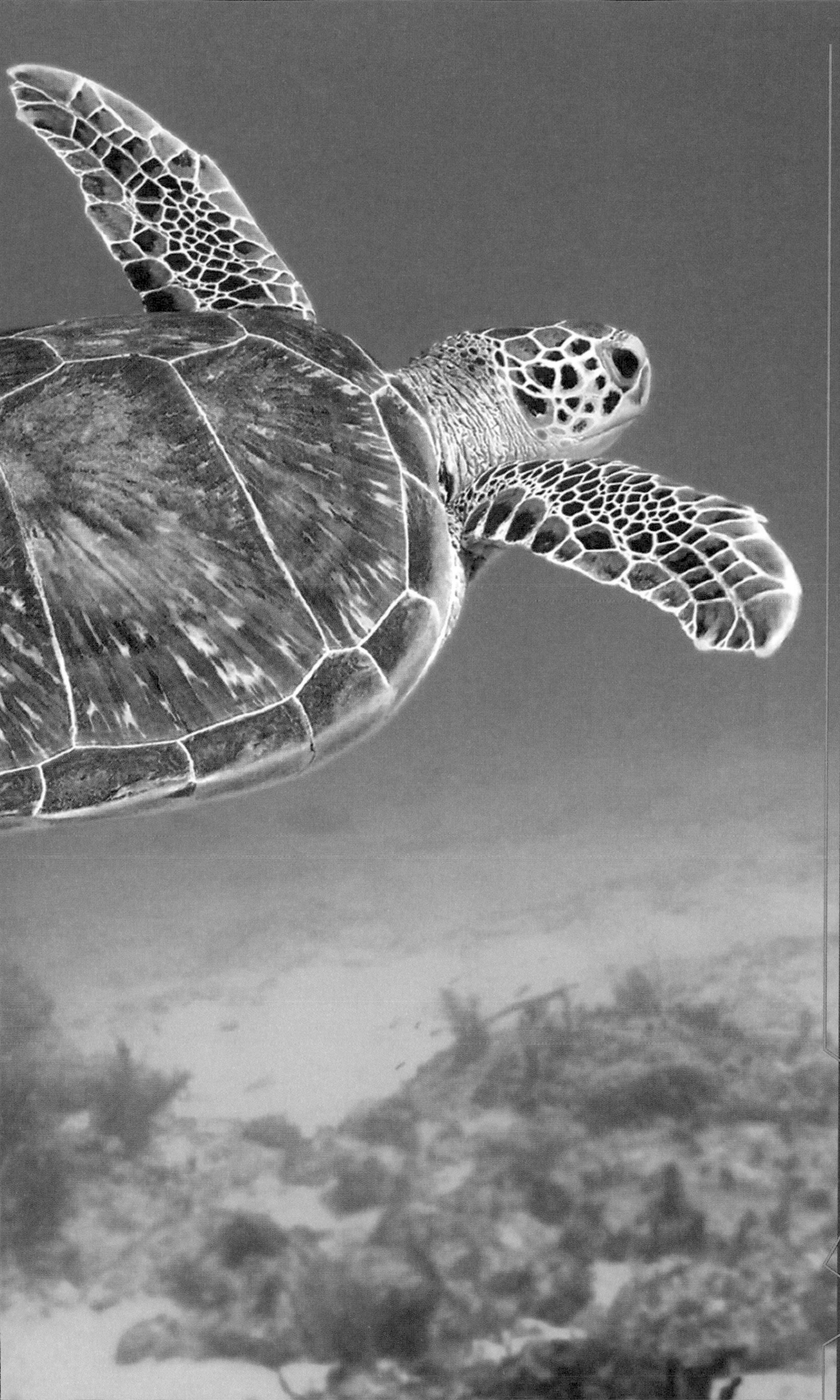

GLOSSARY

adapt—To change to meet the demands of the environment.

captivity—Being in a zoo instead of the wild.

carapace—The upper part of a turtle's shell.

carbon dioxide—A heat-trapping gas given off when fossil fuels are burned.

conservation—The protection of nature and animals.

coral reef—Underwater ridges or structures made of coral, a hard substance made of the skeletons of tiny sea creatures.

ecosystem—The plants and animals in an area interacting with the environment and with each other.

endangered—At risk of becoming extinct.

environment—The natural world; the area in which a person or animal lives.

extinct—Died out completely.

fibropapillomatosis—A disease that causes tumors to grow on marine turtles' bodies.

genus—A group of related animals, often made up of many species.

habitat—The place in which an animal lives; the features of that place including plants, landforms, and weather.

incubate—To develop as an egg.

mutualism—A relationship between two different species that helps both.

organism—A plant or an animal.

plastron—The lower part of a turtle's shell.

poach—To illegally kill or steal protected wild animals.

pollution—Substances in the air and water that harm the environment and animals that live there.

population—The total number of a group of animals.

species—A specific group of animals with shared physical characteristics and genes; members within a species can breed with each other to produce offspring.

FURTHER READING

Books

Cerullo, Mary M., and Jeffrey L. Rotman. *Sea Turtles: Ocean Nomads*. New York: Dalton Children's Books, 2003.

Berkenkamp, Laurie, and Chuck Forsman. *Discover the Oceans: The World's Largest Ecosystem*. White River Junction, VT: Nomad Press, 2009.

Hickman, Pamela. *Turtle Rescue*. Richmond Hill, ON: Firefly Books, 2005.

Kingfisher, Nicola Davies. *Oceans and Seas*. New York: Houghton Mifflin Company, 2007.

Lasky, Kathryn. *Interrupted Journey: Saving Endangered Sea Turtles*. Cambridge, MA: Candlewick Press, 2001.

Internet Addresses

Caribbean Conservation Corporation and Sea Turtle Survival League
<http://www.cccturtle.org>

Sea World Animals: Sea Turtle Infobook
<http://www.seaworld.org/animal-info/info-books/sea-turtle/index.htm>

Tagging of Pacific Predators: Leatherback Turtle
<http://www.topp.org/species/leatherback_turtle>

INDEX